107

 **W9-BDV-015**

Iowa

BY ANN HEINRICHS

Content Adviser: Loren Horton, Ph.D, State Historical Society of Iowa, Iowa City, Iowa

Reading Adviser: Dr. Linda D. Labbo, Department of Reading Education, College of Education, The University of Georgia

COMPASS POINT BOOKS ✦ MINNEAPOLIS, MINNESOTA

Compass Point Books
3109 West 50th Street, #115
Minneapolis, MN 55410

Visit Compass Point Books on the Internet at *www.compasspointbooks.com*
or e-mail your request to *custserv@compasspointbooks.com*

On the cover: Morning light on a farm near Woodbine in Harrison County

Photographs ©: AirPhoto/Jim Wark, cover, 1; Unicorn Stock Photos/Ed Harp, 3, 4; Unicorn Stock
Photos/Martin R. Jones, 6, 45; John Elk III, 8, 9, 20, 36, 43 (top); Corbis/Tom Bean, 10; Greg Lasley/
KAC Productions, 11; Robert McCaw, 12, 44 (top), 48 (top); D. Cavagnaro/Visuals Unlimited, 13;
Ken Martin/Visuals Unlimited, 14; Hulton/Archive by Getty Images, 15, 16, 19, 21, 33, 46; North
Wind Picture Archive, 17, 41; Corbis/Bettmann, 18, 29; Unicorn Stock Photos/Sohm, 22; Unicorn
Stock Photos/Paula J. Harrington, 23, 40; Bruce Leighty/The Image Finders, 25; Eric R. Berndt/The
Image Finders, 26; Unicorn Stock Photos/Jim Shippee, 27; Corbis/Wes Thompson, 28; Rick Poley/
Visuals Unlimited, 30; Unicorn Stock Photos/MacDonald Photography, 31; Unicorn Stock Photos/Gerry
Schnieders, 32; Wagner Photo/The Image Finders, 34; James P. Rowan, 37, 38, 42, 47; Corbis/Michael
S. Lewis, 39; Robesus, Inc., 43 (state flag); One Mile Up, Inc., 43 (state seal); Comstock, 44 (bottom).

Editors: E. Russell Primm, Emily J. Dolbear, and Catherine Neitge
Photo Researcher: Marcie C. Spence
Photo Selector: Linda S. Koutris
Designer/Page Production: The Design Lab/Jaime Martens
Cartographer: XNR Productions, Inc.

Library of Congress Cataloging-in-Publication Data
Heinrichs, Ann.
  Iowa / by Ann Heinrichs.
    p. cm. — (This land is your land)
 Summary: Describes the geography, history, government, people, culture, and attractions of Iowa.
Includes bibliographical references (p.) and index.
  ISBN 0-7565-0342-6 (hardcover : alk. paper)
  1. Iowa—Juvenile literature. [1. Iowa.] I. Title.
  F621.3 .H45 2004
  977.7—dc21   2002151669

Table of Contents

NOTE: In this book, words that are defined in the glossary are in **bold** the first time they appear in the text.

▲ **Dolliver Memorial State Park in Lehigh**

Clarence Anderson is an Iowa farmer. His children urged him to enter the tall-corn contest at the Iowa State Fair. He did—and wound up winning the blue ribbon for the tallest corn. The towering plant stood 14 feet, 8 inches (4½ meters) high. "My goal is 20 feet [6 m]," he says. "Maybe I'll get that next year."

Iowans are proud of their corn—and they should be! Iowa grows more corn than any other state. It's eaten fresh or made into popcorn, cereal, sweeteners for soft drinks, other foods, and even fuel. Corn cobs are used for making plastics. Iowa also exports corn to feed people in countries around the world.

Settlers came from many lands to farm Iowa's rich, black soil. Today, Iowa is one of America's top farming states. Iowa's factories are busy, too. They make food products, farm machines, plastics, and many other goods.

Farmland covers most of Iowa. However, visitors also enjoy the state's woodlands, cliffs, and streams. These natural areas recall the days of Native Americans, explorers, and pioneers. Now come along and explore Iowa, too!

Rolling Hills and Plains

▲ A view of the Mississippi River in McGregor

Iowa is a middle-sized state in America's Midwest region. Twenty-five states are larger than Iowa, and twenty-four are smaller. Iowa is the only state whose east and west borders are formed by water. The Mississippi River creates Iowa's eastern border. The Missouri River forms its western edge.

Iowa's north and south borders are perfectly straight lines. To the north is Minnesota. Missouri borders the south. On the west, across the Missouri River, are South Dakota and Nebraska. Wisconsin and Illinois lie to the east, across the Mississippi.

The Missouri River is actually a tributary, or branch, of the Mississippi. It empties into the Mississippi near Saint Louis, Missouri. Many other rivers run through Iowa. They all flow into either the Mississippi River or the Missouri River. Early explorers and settlers entered Iowa on these rivers. That's why Iowa's major cities are located on riverbanks.

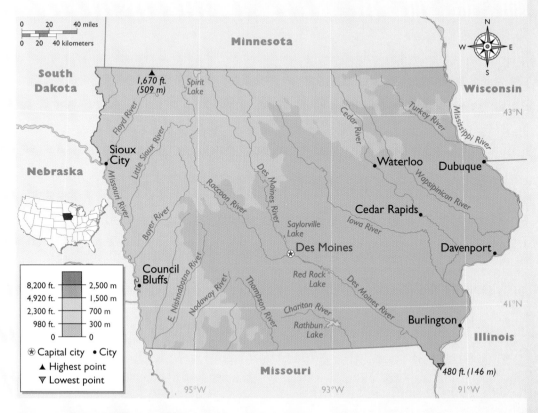

▲ **A topographic map of Iowa**

▲ The skyline along the Des Moines River

Dubuque and Davenport are port cities on the Mississippi River. Des Moines, the state capital, lies on the Des Moines River. Cedar Rapids and Waterloo stand beside the Cedar River. On Iowa's western border, Sioux City overlooks the Missouri River.

Glaciers, or huge sheets of ice, once covered Iowa. Over thousands of years, these glaciers moved across the land. Their movements created the landscape you see in Iowa today.

Flat or rolling plains cover northern and central Iowa. Here the glaciers left a smooth, level surface. As they melted, they left rich materials that broke down to become soil. That soil is now fertile farmland. The melting glaciers also created **swamps** and lakes. Farmers in the 1800s drained the swamps to create more farmland. Many small lakes remain, though.

▲ This farm is one of many in northern Iowa.

Southern and western Iowa are not as flat as other regions. They have rolling hills and rocky **ridges.** The glaciers left rich deposits here, too. Later, however, many streams cut through the land. They carved out the ridges and hills. High **bluffs** overlook the Missouri River in some spots.

Iowa's roughest landscape is the northeast, along the Mississippi River. Very little glacier movement took place here.

▲ **Hanging Rock at Effigy Mounds National Monument is part of Iowa's rough landscape along the Mississippi River.**

▲ **Coyotes roam Iowa's plains.**

The land is rugged, with many forested hills. Rocky bluffs rise along the river.

Iowa's forests give shelter to deer, foxes, rabbits, and other creatures. Pheasants, partridges, and quails nest in tall grasses across the prairies and plains. Coyotes also roam across the plains.

▲ Ducks are a common sight in Iowa in spring and fall.

Huge flocks of ducks, geese, and other birds pass through in the spring and fall. They are migrating, or traveling, between northern and southern feeding grounds. How do they find their way? They follow the Mississippi and Missouri Rivers, which they see from high in the sky. They stop to rest and eat in Iowa on their way.

Iowa's summers are warm and sunny. Once in a while, though, temperatures can get blazing hot. Droughts, or lack of rain, sometimes make farmers' crops wither and die. Most parts of Iowa get heavy winter snowfalls. High winds often whip across the plains. They create fierce **blizzards** and bone-chilling temperatures.

▲ **A snowy winter at Heritage Farm in Decorah**

▲ These Indian Mounds are located in Toolesboro.

People lived in Iowa thousands of years ago. They hunted mammoths and other **prehistoric** animals. Later, people called the Mound Builders lived in the region. They built huge mounds, or piles of earth and stone. Many of these mounds were built in the shape of animals.

European explorers found many Native Americans in what is now Iowa. In the east, along the Mississippi River, were the Ioway, Illini, and Sioux. The Omaha, Oto, and Missouri people lived in the west. They raised corn and hunted bison (buffalo) across the plains.

French explorers from Canada were the first white people to reach this area. Louis Joliet and Father Jacques Marquette canoed down the Mississippi River in 1673. On the way, they landed on Iowa's shores. In 1682, René-Robert Cavelier, Sieur de La Salle, explored the Mississippi. He claimed the entire Mississippi River Valley for France. This included present-day Iowa. La Salle named this vast region Louisiana, after King Louis XIV of France.

▲ **A member of the Ioway tribe**

▲ **René-Robert Cavelier, Sieur de La Salle**

Fur traders and Roman Catholic **missionaries** entered Iowa in the 1700s. In 1788, Julien Dubuque and a group of lead miners settled near today's city of Dubuque. That became Iowa's first town.

The United States bought France's Louisiana colony in 1803. Meriwether Lewis and William Clark were sent to explore this new land. They passed through Iowa on the Missouri River in 1804 and in 1806.

Many events shaped Iowa over the next years. More and more settlers wanted Native American lands west of the Mississippi River. In 1832, Americans defeated the Native Americans in the

▲ **Fur traders came to Iowa in the 1700s.**

▲ **Native Americans fought to keep their land along the Mississippi during the Black Hawk War.**

Black Hawk War. As a result, settlers gained a strip of land along the Mississippi River in eastern Iowa. Through treaties or wars, settlers eventually pushed most of the Native Americans out.

In 1838, Iowa Territory was created. It included present-day Iowa and parts of Minnesota, North Dakota, and South Dakota. In 1846, Iowa became the twenty-ninth state in the Union.

The new state grew quickly as thousands of new settlers arrived. Many grew corn, wheat, and potatoes in Iowa's rich soil. Some raised cattle and hogs, fattening them on Iowa corn. Others worked in sawmills along the Mississippi River. People built houses with lumber from the sawmills.

Meanwhile, Northern and Southern states fiercely disagreed about slavery. This led to the Civil War (1861–1865). Some Iowans had slaves, but most people in the state were against slavery. Iowa fought on the Northern, or Union, side, which opposed slavery. In the end, the Union forces won.

New railroads made a big difference for Iowans after the war. Cattle and hog farmers could ship their beef and pork to faraway cities. Many Iowa cities became important **meat-packing** centers.

▲ A railroad station in North McGregor in 1870

▲ Men waiting in line to get a meal at a Dubuque mission during the Great Depression

Iowa farmers suffered many ups and downs over the years. Crop prices dropped, and many farmers found themselves in debt. Railroads charged high prices, too. Farmers joined an organization called the National Grange. Through the Grange, they were able to get lower shipping costs.

Luckily, prices for farm products rose in the early 1900s. However, prices for farmland rose, too. Many farmers borrowed money to buy land. Then they lost their land because they couldn't pay back those loans. To make matters worse, the Great Depression hit hard in the 1930s. Like people around the

▲ This coal power plant is located in Allamakee County.

country, thousands of Iowans lost their jobs and homes. World War II (1939–1945) made a big difference for Iowa's farmers. They sold tons of corn and meat to feed American troops.

Many new factories opened in Iowa after the war. They made foods, metal goods, farm machinery, and many other products. By the mid-1970s, manufacturing brought more income into Iowa than farming. Still, Iowa depends heavily on agriculture. State leaders are working hard to bring more businesses into the state.

Iowans have always taken an active part in their government. Iowa farmers gained a strong voice in their state government in the 1870s. During the Great Depression, farmers again got their state lawmakers to pass helpful laws. One Iowan even became president of the United States. It was Herbert Hoover, who was born in West Branch. He was president from 1929 to 1933.

▲ **Former president Herbert Hoover was born in West Branch.**

Iowa's state government works much like the U.S. government. It is organized into three branches—legislative, executive, and judicial. These three branches make for a good balance of governing power.

▲ The state capitol in Des Moines

The legislative branch makes the state's laws. Iowans elect their lawmakers to serve in the general assembly. It has two houses, or sections. One is the 50-member senate. The other is the 100-member house of representatives. They all meet in the state capitol in Des Moines.

The executive branch makes sure people obey the laws. Iowa's governor is the state's chief executive. Voters elect him or her to a four-year term. Some states limit their governor's number of terms, but Iowans can elect the same governor any number of times.

Judges and their courts make up the judicial branch. The judges know a lot about state and national laws. They hear the cases of people accused of breaking the law. Iowa's

▲ **The Dubuque County Courthouse**

supreme court is the state's highest court. The governor appoints its seven judges, or justices.

Iowa is divided into ninety-nine counties. Each one is governed by a board of supervisors. Iowa's counties may choose to have home rule. That means they can draw up their own charters, or basic rules. Cities are governed by a mayor or manager and a city council. Iowa's cities may also choose home rule.

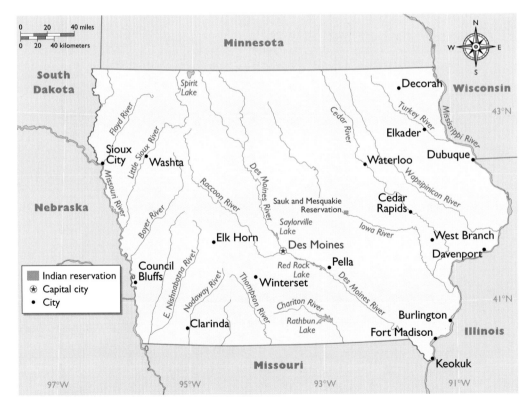

▲ **A geopolitical map of Iowa**

Iowans at Work

▲ A cornfield in Dyersville

One day in 2002, an Iowa farmer decided to measure the corn in his cornfield. He found that most of his plants stood 11 feet (3⅓ m) high. That's probably taller than the room you are sitting in right now!

Many Iowa farmers have produced even taller corn. When it comes to growing corn, Iowa is a champion. One out of every five bushels of corn in the nation comes from Iowa.

Almost everywhere you go in Iowa, you see farms. Iowa's rich, black soil makes it a leading farm state. Only California and Texas have a higher farm income than Iowa. Iowa ranks first in corn and soybeans, as well as hogs and pigs. Hogs are the most important farm animals. In fact, Iowa produces about one out of every four hogs in the country! Iowa farmers also raise beef and dairy cattle, oats, hay, cabbage, and apples.

Most manufacturing in Iowa is related to farming. Food products are the state's top factory goods. Food plants process corn, pork, oats, milk, and many other farm products.

▲ **A hog farm in southwestern Iowa**

They make foods such as sausage, butter, and oatmeal. Quaker Oats, which started in Cedar Rapids, is one of the world's largest cereal companies. What about Iowa's famous corn? It's made into popcorn, corn oil, corn syrup, cornmeal, and fuel called ethanol.

▲ Quaker Oats got its start in Cedar Rapids.

Other factories make farm equipment such as tractors and harvesting machines. Chemicals are important factory products, too. They include fertilizer and medicines.

More than two out of every three Iowa workers hold service jobs. Many work for insurance companies located in Des Moines. Others are health care workers in Iowa's many medical centers. Stores, schools, repair shops, and banks all employ service workers to make their businesses run smoothly.

▲ Service workers are important to insurance companies like Employers Mutual in Des Moines.

You may have seen a famous picture that was painted in Iowa. It shows a plain-looking man and woman standing in front of a farmhouse. The man is holding a pitchfork. This painting is *American Gothic,* by Iowa artist Grant Wood. Some people say the couple looks grumpy, unfriendly, or sad. However, Wood meant only to show people from a typical small town.

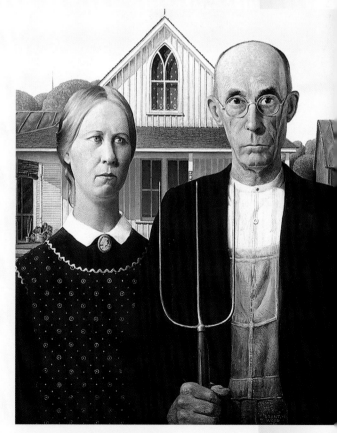

Many small towns spread across Iowa's landscape. Until the 1950s, most Iowans lived in rural areas. Those are areas outside of cities and towns. Since then, however, many people have left their farms for city jobs. Des Moines, the state capital, is the largest city.

▲ **Iowa artist Grant Wood painted *American Gothic.***

Next in size are Cedar Rapids, Davenport, and Sioux City. Almost 3 million people lived in Iowa in 2000. That made Iowa number thirty in population among the fifty states.

At first, most new settlers in Iowa came from other states. After about 1850, **immigrants** began arriving from European countries. The largest group came from what is now Germany. Others came from Ireland and Wales. In the late 1800s, many people arrived from Norway, Sweden, and Denmark. Other European settlers to arrive were Dutch, Czech, Slovak, Croatian,

▲ Although many Iowans have city jobs, many others still own farms.

▲ **A post office in West Amana**

and Italian. People with **Hispanic,** African-American, and Asian roots live in Iowa, too.

A German religious group founded the Amana Colonies in the 1850s. Today, these colonies include seven villages in eastern Iowa. Villagers farm and make clothing, furniture, and appliances.

Many events reflect Iowa's farming **culture.** The Iowa State Fair in Des Moines is one of America's largest state fairs. Proud farmers display their fattest cattle and hogs and their biggest vegetables. Clay County holds a huge agricultural fair, too. Cowboys show off their skills in Fort Madison's Tri-State Rodeo.

Other festivals celebrate Iowa's diverse cultures. The Amana Colonies hold an Oktoberfest in the fall. The Dutch community in Pella holds a tulip festival in May. People dress in traditional Dutch costumes, complete with wooden shoes. Decorah's three-day Nordic Fest celebrates the town's Norwegian **heritage.** The Meskwaki Indians hold a powwow on the Tama Settlement in late summer. Czech, Danish, Swedish, Italian, and many other groups have their own festivals, too.

▲ **Children in traditional Dutch dress at Pella's tulip festival**

▲ Glenn Miller playing his trombone

Glenn Miller was one of the most popular bandleaders of the 1930s and 1940s. Now Clarinda, his birthplace, holds an international Glenn Miller Festival every year. The Bix Beiderbecke Memorial Jazz Festival takes place in Davenport. Beiderbecke, a Davenport native, was one of the world's greatest cornet players.

▲ The University of Iowa's football team, the Hawkeyes

Iowans enjoy plenty of sports action. The Iowa Cubs play baseball in Des Moines. They are the top minor-league team of the Chicago Cubs. Football and basketball fans pack the stadiums and arenas at Iowa's state universities in Ames, Iowa City, and Cedar Falls. Drake University holds a track-and-field competition every April. Iowa's high schoolers are active in sports, too. Huge crowds show up for the girls' and boys' high school basketball tournaments every year.

From the air, you can see the grand design of Effigy Mounds. You can see the shapes of birds, bears, reptiles, and other creatures. Prehistoric people built these mounds hundreds of years ago. A tour on foot is exciting, too. More than two hundred mounds remain at the site.

Many of Iowa's early settlers came from faraway countries.

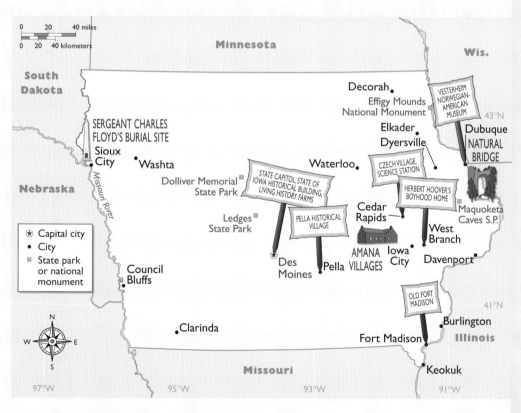

0   20   40 miles
0   20   40 kilometers

Minnesota

Wis.

South Dakota

SERGEANT CHARLES FLOYD'S BURIAL SITE

Decorah

Effigy Mounds National Monument

VESTERHEIM NORWEGIAN-AMERICAN MUSEUM

43°N

Elkader

Dyersville

Dubuque

NATURAL BRIDGE

Sioux City

Washta

Waterloo

CZECH VILLAGE, SCIENCE STATION

Nebraska

Missouri River

Dolliver Memorial State Park

STATE CAPITOL, STATE OF IOWA HISTORICAL BUILDING, LIVING HISTORY FARMS

HERBERT HOOVER'S BOYHOOD HOME

Maquoketa Caves S.P.

Ledges State Park

PELLA HISTORICAL VILLAGE

Cedar Rapids

West Branch

Capital city
City
State park or national monument

Council Bluffs

Des Moines

Pella

AMANA VILLAGES

Iowa City

Davenport

OLD FORT MADISON

41°N

N
W   E
S

Clarinda

Fort Madison

Burlington

Illinois

Keokuk

Missouri

97°W   95°W   93°W   91°W

▲ Places to visit in Iowa

Their cultures are still alive in Iowa today. People in the Amana villages near Cedar Rapids sell their handmade crafts. Historic buildings in each village show how the Amana colonists lived in the 1850s.

Czech Village in Cedar Rapids has many historic shops and bakeries. Dutch culture comes to life at Pella Historical Village near Des Moines. Among the village's twenty-one steep-roofed Dutch buildings are a school and a store. The Vesterheim Norwegian-American Museum in Decorah includes a log schoolhouse, an old stone mill, and an immigrant museum.

▲ Furniture inside the Vesterheim Norwegian-American Museum

▲ Replicas of the original buildings can be seen at Old Fort Madison.

A high dome towers over the state capitol in Des Moines. Inside, you'll find a collection of battle flags—and the state lawmakers at work. Nearby is the State of Iowa Historical Building.

Costumed soldiers and their families are your guides at Old Fort Madison. Craftspeople demonstrate baking, candle dipping, and musket firing. You'll take another step back in time at the Living History Farms near Des Moines. There you'll learn about Native American crop growing, pioneers' ox-drawn plows, and early iron farm machines. You'll also visit a bustling Iowa frontier town. Chat with the blacksmiths, cabinetmakers, and other merchants. They explain how their shops served the surrounding farm families.

Jesse Hoover was a pioneer blacksmith in West Branch, near Iowa City. His son Herbert became president of the United States. Today, visitors can tour Herbert's boyhood home. Nearby are Hoover's presidential museum and library.

How would you like to be inside a huge bubble? Or be a television weather reporter? Or conduct your own science experiments? The Science Station in Cedar Rapids lets you do all this and more. It has more than one hundred hands-on science exhibits.

▲ **Herbert Hoover was born in this house in West Branch.**

▲ Spirit Lake is one of a chain of lakes in Iowa's resort region near the Minnesota border.

Sergeant Charles Floyd was the only member of the Lewis and Clark expedition to die on the journey. His burial site is on Floyd's Bluff in Sioux City. At Council Bluffs, Lewis and Clark held an important meeting with Native Americans.

Although Iowa is mostly farmland, it also has beautiful lakes and many wild, natural areas. Hiking trails in these areas lead through thick forests teeming with wildlife. In Ledges State Park, visitors can take a scenic train ride overlooking the Des Moines Valley. High sandstone cliffs tower over the forests in Dolliver Memorial State Park. Some cliffs were worn away by ancient rivers more than 150 million years ago. You can also

▲ One of the many caves in Maquoketa Caves State Park

view Indian burial mounds and Bone Yard Hollow, a ravine where buffalo were once hunted.

Maquoketa Caves near Dubuque are a network of haunting underground caves. You can tour many of them. Nature walks in the area lead past Natural Bridge and the 17-ton Balanced Rock. These wonders were as awesome to Iowa's ancient people as they are to you today. They make Iowa a great place to explore.

Important Dates

1673 Explorers Louis Joliet and Father Jacques Marquette travel down the Mississippi River.

1682 René-Robert Cavelier, Sieur de La Salle, claims the Mississippi River Valley, including Iowa, for France.

1803 In the Louisiana Purchase, Iowa passes from France to the United States.

1832 The U.S. Army defeats Native Americans in the Black Hawk War.

1836 Iowa becomes part of Wisconsin Territory.

1838 Iowa Territory is created.

1846 Iowa becomes the twenty-ninth U.S. state on December 28.

1867 A new railroad opens across all of Iowa.

1913 The Keokuk Dam opens.

1929 Herbert Hoover of West Branch becomes the thirty-first U.S. president.

1970s Manufacturing replaces farming as Iowa's leading source of income.

1993 Floods cause massive damage to Iowa farms and property.

1999 Terry Branstad completes his fourth four-year term as Iowa's governor and holds the record for serving the most years in that office.

Glossary

blizzards—winter storms created by high winds

bluffs—high, often rocky, cliffs

culture—groups of people who share beliefs, customs, and a way of life

heritage—customs and beliefs passed down through many generations

immigrants—people who come to another country to live

meat-packing—the business of slaughtering animals in large numbers and preparing their meat to be sold to markets and butcher shops

missionaries—people who travel to teach religion

prehistoric—existing before people began to record history

ridges—long, narrow strips of high land or rocks

swamps—wet, spongy land

Did You Know?

★ Dakota Sioux Indians called a related group Ioway or Iowa. It meant "sleepy ones" in the Dakota language. Early French explorers named the Iowa River after these people. The territory of Iowa was named after the river.

★ Spirit Lake is Iowa's largest glacier-made lake.

★ Herbert Hoover was the first U.S. president to be born west of the Mississippi River.

★ Campers and motor homes called Winnebagos are made in Iowa's Winnebago County.

★ Iowa is the only state whose name begins with two vowels.

★ Iowa's nickname is The Hawkeye State. It is believed that the name honors the Native American chief Black Hawk.

★ Elk Horn, Iowa, is the nation's largest rural settlement of Danish people.

State capital: Des Moines

State motto: Our Liberties We Prize and Our Rights We Will Maintain.

State nickname: The Hawkeye State

Statehood: December 28, 1846; twenty-ninth state

Land area: 55,875 square miles (144,716 sq km); **rank:** twenty-third

Highest point: In northern Osceola County, 1,670 feet (509 m)

Lowest point: In Lee County where the Des Moines and Mississippi Rivers meet, 480 feet (146 m)

Highest recorded temperature: 118°F (48°C) at Keokuk on July 20, 1934

Lowest recorded temperature: −47°F (−44°C) at Washta on January 12, 1912, and at Elkader on February 3, 1996

Average January temperature: 19°F (−7°C)

Average July temperature: 75°F (24°C)

Population in 2000: 2,926,324; **rank:** thirtieth

Largest cities in 2000: Des Moines (198,682), Cedar Rapids (120,758), Davenport (98,359), Sioux City (85,013)

Factory products: Foods, farm machines, electrical equipment, chemicals

Farm products: Corn, hogs, beef cattle, soybeans, milk

Mining products: Limestone, sand, gravel

State flag: Iowa's state flag has three

wide, vertical stripes—blue, white, and red. The blue stripe stands for loyalty, justice, and truth. The white stripe represents purity, and the red stripe stands for courage. In the center is an eagle holding a banner in its beak. On the banner is the state motto, "Our Liberties We Prize and Our Rights We Will Maintain." Beneath the eagle is the word *Iowa* in red letters.

State seal: The state seal shows a citi-

zen-soldier standing in a wheat field and holding an American flag. Around him are farming and industrial tools. They stand for Iowa's agriculture and industry. The Mississippi River, Iowa's greatest river, flows in the background. Overhead is an eagle with a banner in its beak. As on the state flag, the banner shows the state motto.

State abbreviations: Iowa or Ia. (traditional); IA (postal)

State Symbols

State bird: Eastern goldfinch

State flower: Wild rose

State tree: Oak

State rock: Geode

Making Chocolate Chip-Oatmeal Cookies

Oats are one of Iowa's great farm products!

Makes about twenty-four cookies.

INGREDIENTS:

½ cup margarine

½ cup brown sugar, packed

½ cup granulated sugar

1 egg

½ teaspoon vanilla

1 cup flour

1 teaspoon baking soda

¼ teaspoon salt

2 cups uncooked oatmeal

¾ cup chocolate chips

¾ cup chopped nuts

DIRECTIONS:

Make sure an adult helps you with the hot oven. Preheat the oven to 350°F.

Mix the margarine and sugars in a bowl until the mixture is creamy. Beat in the egg and vanilla. In another bowl, mix the flour, baking soda, and salt. Stir it into the sugar mixture. Stir in the oatmeal, chocolate chips, and nuts. Grease a cookie sheet.

Drop heaping teaspoonfuls of the dough onto the cookie sheet, about two inches apart. Bake for 10 minutes. Cool on a wire rack.

"Song of Iowa"

Words by S. H. M. Byers, sung to the tune of the traditional Christmas song "O Tannenbaum"

You asked what land I love the best, Iowa,
'tis Iowa,
The fairest State of all the west, Iowa,
O! Iowa.
From yonder Mississippi's stream
To where Missouri's waters gleam
O! fair it is as poet's dream, Iowa, in Iowa.

See yonder fields of tasseled corn, Iowa,
in Iowa,
Where plenty fills her golden horn, Iowa,
in Iowa.
See how her wondrous prairies shine
To yonder sunset's purpling line.
O! Happy land, O! land of mine, Iowa,
O! Iowa.

And she has maids whose laughing eyes,
Iowa, O! Iowa.
To him who loves were Paradise, Iowa,
O! Iowa.
O! happiest fate that e'er was known.
Such eyes to shine for one alone,
To call such beauty all his own. Iowa,
O! Iowa.

Go read the story of thy past, Iowa,
O! Iowa.
What glorious deeds, what fame thou hast!
Iowa, O! Iowa.
So long as time's great cycle runs,
Or nations weep their fallen ones,
Thou'lt not forget thy patriot sons, Iowa,
O! Iowa.

Carrie Chapman Catt (1859–1947) played a leading role in the struggle to get women the right to vote. She also founded the League of Women Voters. She was born in Wisconsin and moved to Iowa as a child. She graduated from what is now Iowa State University.

William "Buffalo Bill" Cody (1846–1917) was a frontier scout and expert marksman. He founded Buffalo Bill's Wild West Show, which toured the United States and Europe. Cody was born in Scott County.

Lee De Forest (1873–1961) was an inventor whose work led to the invention of the radio. He was born in Council Bluffs.

Herbert Hoover (1874–1964) was the thirty-first U.S. president (1929–1933). He was born in West Branch.

Ann Landers (1918–2002) wrote a popular newspaper advice column. She was the twin sister of columnist Abigail Van Buren "Dear Abby." She was born Esther Friedman in Sioux City.

Glenn Miller (1904–1944) was a bandleader and composer. His Glenn Miller Orchestra was one of the most popular bands of the 1930s and 1940s. "In the Mood" and "Little Brown Jug" were two of his many compositions. Miller (pictured above left) was born in Clarinda.

Harry Reasoner (1923–1991) was a television news broadcaster and host of the news show *60 Minutes*. He was born in Dakota City.

Donna Reed (1921–1986) was an actress. Her movies include *It's a Wonderful Life* (1946) and *From Here to Eternity* (1953). She also hosted her own television series, *The Donna Reed Show*. She was born Donna Belle Mullenger in Denison.

Lillian Russell (1861–1922) was a singer in both operas and popular musicals. She was born Helen Louise Leonard in Clinton.

Wallace Stegner (1909–1993) was a novelist who wrote about life in the American West. He was born in Lake Mills.

Abigail Van Buren (1918–) wrote the newspaper advice column "Dear Abby." She is the twin sister of the late columnist Ann Landers. She was born Pauline Friedman in Sioux City.

John Wayne (1907–1979) was an actor known for his tough cowboy roles. He appeared in more than two hundred movies. He was born Marion Michael Morrison in Winterset.

Meredith Willson (1902–1984) was the author and composer of the Broadway musical *The Music Man*. He was born in Mason City.

Grant Wood (1892–1942) was an artist who painted ordinary people of the Midwest. His best-known painting is *American Gothic*. Wood was born in Anamosa.

At the Library

Balcavage, Dynise. *Iowa*. Danbury, Conn.: Children's Press, 2002.

Edwards, Michelle. *Eve and Smithy: An Iowa Tale*. New York: Lothrop Lee & Shepard, 1994.

Gensicke, Mary Ann, and Lonna Nachtigal (illustrator). *I Is for Iowa*. Ames: Iowa State University Press, 1995.

LaDoux, Rita. *Iowa*. Minneapolis: Lerner, 2002.

Thompson, Kathleen. *Iowa*. Austin, Tex.: Raintree/Steck-Vaughn, 1996.

Welsbacher, Anne. *Iowa*. Edina, Minn.: Abdo & Daughters, 1998.

On the Web

Iowa State Web site

http://www.state.ia.us/
To learn about Iowa's history, government, economy, and land

Iowa: Come Be Our Guest

http://www.traveliowa.com
To find out about Iowa's events, activities, and places to visit

Through the Mail

Public Information Office

General Assembly
Iowa State Capitol
East 12th and Grand
Des Moines, IA 50319
For information about Iowa's economy, government, and history

Iowa Department of Economic Development

Iowa Tourism Office
200 East Grand Avenue
Des Moines, IA 50309
For information on travel and interesting sights in Iowa

On the Road

Iowa State Capitol

East 12th and Grand
Des Moines, IA 50319
515/281-5591
To visit Iowa's state capitol

State of Iowa Historical Building

600 East Locust
Des Moines, IA 50319
515/281-5111
To explore Iowa's history

Index

About the Author

Ann Heinrichs grew up in Fort Smith, Arkansas, and lives in Chicago. She is the author of more than one hundred books for children and young adults on Asian, African, and U.S. history and culture. Ann has also written numerous newspaper, magazine, and encyclopedia articles. She is an award-winning martial artist, specializing in t'ai chi empty-hand and sword forms.

Ann has traveled widely throughout the United States, Africa, Asia, and the Middle East. In exploring each state for this series, she rediscovered the people, history, and resources that make this a great land, as well as the concerns we share with people around the world.